HUGGER TO THE RESCUE

DOROTHY HINSHAW PATENT

PHOTOGRAPHS BY
WILLIAM MUÑOZ

Someone is lost in the woods. He might be hurt, or the weather may turn bad. It is important to find him quickly. Call in the search and rescue dogs!

Here are Hugger, Panda, Chelsie, and Hydra — all members of Black Paws Search, Rescue & Avalanche Dogs team. Although they are pets as well, the dogs have received special training to help them in rescue work in forests, snow, and in the water.

Wearing their special uniforms, carrying first aid materials for both dog and victim and other equipment, these Newfoundlands are a welcome sight to anyone lost or injured.

HUGGER
TO THE
RESCUE

DOROTHY HINSHAW PATENT

PHOTOGRAPHS BY
WILLIAM MUÑOZ

COBBLEHILL BOOKS / DUTTON

NEW YORK

For all those involved in search and rescue work,
with our deepest admiration.

ACKNOWLEDGMENTS

The author and photographer wish to thank Susie and Murphy
Foley and the other members of Black Paws Search, Rescue &
Avalanche Dogs for all their help with this project.

Text copyright ©1994 by Dorothy Hinshaw Patent
Photographs copyright ©1994 by William Muñoz

Library of Congress Cataloging-in-Publication Data
Patent, Dorothy Hinshaw.
Hugger to the rescue / Dorothy Hinshaw Patent; photographs by William Muñoz.
p.   cm.
ISBN 0-525-65161-6
1. Rescue dogs—Juvenile literature.   2. Search dogs—Juvenile literature.
3. Newfoundland dog—Juvenile literature.   4.Search and rescue operations—Juvenile
literature. [1. Rescue dogs.   2. Search dogs.   3. Newfoundland dog.   4. Rescue work.]
I. Muñoz, William, ill.   II. Title.
SF428.55.P37   1994
636.7'088'6—dc20   93–32031   CIP   AC

Published in the United States by Cobblehill Books,
an affiliate of Dutton Children's Books,
a division of Penguin USA Inc.,
375 Hudson Street, New York, New York 10014

Designed by Joseph Rutt

Printed in Hong Kong   First Edition
10 9 8 7 6 5 4 3 2 1

Panda and Susie are set to search.

Someone is lost in the woods. He might be hurt, or the weather could turn bad. It is important to find him as fast as possible. But he didn't follow a trail, and footprints don't show on the forest floor. What to do?

Call in the search and rescue dogs. Dogs have a very fine sense of smell. They can find people lost by following their scents, because each person has his or her own, unique scent.

Panda sniffs clothing belonging to the person playing "lost" during a training session.

Now Panda is ready to go.

Panda is a Newfoundland dog trained to locate lost people. She and her owner, Susie Foley, know how to search through the woods, under the snow, or in the water. Sometimes a piece of the lost person's clothing is available for the dog to smell. But even without knowing the special scent, a trained dog knows to sniff the air, searching for the smell of a human.

Panda catches the scent and off she goes. She checks the ground if she loses the odor trail in the air. Once she finds the lost person, she licks him happily. Finding him is her best reward.

She searches . . .

finds the "victim," and shows him to Susie.

Search and rescue dogs work around the world to find lost hunters, hikers, and children. They are called in after avalanches to find people buried in the snow. After earthquakes, they look for people hidden in the rubble. Thousands of people owe their lives to these wonderful animals.

Many breeds of dogs are used for search and rescue. But most require a great deal of training to learn the work. Newfoundlands, however, are special. They have natural lifesaving instincts, so they learn their work quickly.

Dogs like Indigo can find avalanche victims in the snow quickly.

Newfoundland puppies are born with the instinct to find lost people.

Newfoundlands are natural swimmers and love the water.

The Newfoundland — called a "Newfie" or "Newf" for short — originated on Newfoundland Island in Canada. It was developed as a working dog that performed a variety of tasks like pulling carts and carrying heavy loads. The breed was most useful as a fisherman's companion, for Newfoundlands are as much at home in the water as on dry land. Their webbed feet help them swim, and their thick coats protect them from the icy cold of northern seas.

But saving people is the Newfie's greatest natural talent. Even without training, they will rescue people. During storms, Newfies may patrol the shore. When there have been shipwrecks, Newfies have rescued people without being trained to do so. Newfoundlands are famous for their rescuing skills, especially in water. They have carried lifelines to sinking ships and pulled countless drowning people to shore. A single untrained Newfoundland dog saved a hundred people in one rescue. The water was too rough for rescue boats, but just one dog was able to do the job.

A dog has to be big to perform such work. Newfoundlands weigh from 100 to 160 pounds. They have heavy, muscular bodies and large heads. Most Newfoundlands are black. But they can also be brown, gray, or white and black. They are gentle, good-natured dogs that have a natural love for people.

Hugger is big, even for a Newfie.

Newfies make fine family pets. But such a huge dog is a big responsibility. It needs lots of food. A Newfoundland will eat twenty pounds of dry dog food each week, along with five pounds of meat. In addition, it can consume a pound of rawhide treats and two pounds of dog biscuits. Even with all that food, it will still enjoy table scraps and soup bones for chewing.

Newfs are good family pets that are gentle with children.

Susie Foley with Panda and Hugger.

Susie and Murphy Foley of Bigfork, Montana, raise and train Newfoundland dogs. Their animals are family pets that have a special job. Their volunteer organization, called "Black Paws Search, Rescue & Avalanche Dogs," has chapter groups sprinkled throughout the United States and in other countries. There are two good reasons for the name. Most Newfies do have black fur on their paws. But because of their love of wet places, all Newfoundlands are likely to have "black paws" any time they have a chance to get their feet muddy.

Chelsie is a good mother as well as a fine searcher.

Susie and Murphy use several dogs in their work. Chelsie is a black female. She is loving and obedient, but she is also very determined to do things her way. When she finds a conscious victim, the searchers know right away because they can usually hear the person protesting her enthusiastic dog kisses.

Panda is white and black. Newfoundlands with this special color pattern are called "Landseers." Panda is huge, happy, and especially loyal to Susie. Only when she is at work looking for lost people does she willingly leave Susie's side.

Panda is always enthusiastic about her work.

ABOVE: *Hydra will soon be out searching with the other dogs.*

RIGHT: *Hugger enjoying the sunshine.*

Hydra is just a puppy, but she is learning quickly how to become a fine search and rescue dog. She is curious and lively. Hydra acts as if she really wishes she could talk, she seems so eager to communicate with people.

Hugger, as his name suggests, is calm and lovable. He is especially eager to please, and his large size gives him extra strength that can come in handy in a challenging search. All these dogs, however, are really "huggers" — they love people and enjoy human companionship.

Even though they may rescue people without being taught, Newfoundland dogs need training. So do their human handlers. The dog must learn some important commands. The command "Wait" tells the dog to stop and wait for its handler to catch up — four legs work much better than two on rough or steep ground. If the dog gets distracted by wildlife or the tempting cool water of a creek, it must know to obey and get back to work when its handler calls out, "Leave it."

BELOW: *Susie and Bill Weppler, a Black Paws member, get ready to work with the dogs.*

RIGHT: *Search and rescue dogs often work ahead of their handlers, so voice commands are important.*

Hugger and Susie know how to communicate with one another.

Meanwhile, the handler must get into top physical condition — searching is very hard work! He or she also needs to learn how to "read" the dog — how to know what the dog is trying to tell its handler. Each dog may have its own ways of "alerting" when it makes a find. The type of alert may vary, too, depending on whether the victim responds to the dog or not. For example, when Hugger finds a conscious victim, he wags his tail and waits to be invited over. But if the person is unresponsive, Hugger gives a "woof" while looking at Susie if she is nearby, then another woof. When he sees that she is coming to join him, he woofs one more time.

From the time they are very young, Newfies become used to humans and their gadgets.

Susie plays "hide and seek" with Hydra, a good game for search and rescue training.

Training is best started when the dog is still young. Around eight weeks of age, a puppy is eager to learn and quite unafraid of the unfamiliar. This is a good time to accustom it to situations that might be frightening later on. The puppy and its handler need to get acquainted by playing together, and cuddling creates a special bond. It is also important to become comfortable around other dogs.

Love and kisses bond a puppy to its handler.

Puppies and older dogs enjoy one another's company.

19

ABOVE: *Hydra gets her reward of loving attention for finding Sean during training.*

RIGHT: *Hugger is all ready to go.*

Even a Newfie puppy knows how to follow a human scent and locate a person. It is important to give the puppy practice in searching and to reward success with plenty of praise and petting.

Black Paws' dogs must get used to wearing a uniform. The uniform is a very important part of their work. It carries first aid materials for both the dog and the victim, headlamps for work in the dark, dog cookies, and a canine energy drink.

BELOW: *The uniform is an important piece of equipment.*

The uniform has a harness used when the animal needs to be hoisted by helicopter or rope. The harness straps are tucked into pockets on the uniform when not in use to keep them out of the way. When Susie puts a uniform on one of her dogs, it gets excited. It recognizes the call of duty.

The harness straps are taken from their pockets when they are needed.

ABOVE: *Murphy helps Sooner cross a ravine using a rope. This is called "rappelling."*

RIGHT: *Sooner is calm; he knows Murphy won't let him get hurt.*

23

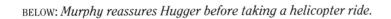

RIGHT: *The two friends ride together.*

The Newfies also need training for water rescue. They need to get used to riding in a boat and to signaling where a person is underwater when they catch the scent in the air. One way a dog can show the right spot is by leaning over and biting at the water. Then divers know to search in that spot.

The dogs must learn how to search from boats.

Trying to locate the scent.

Here it is!

Susie and Panda lead the crowd on the chair lift during a training session.

For avalanche work, the dog needs to become used to riding on a chair lift which might be swaying in the wind. The dog must climb onto the lift willingly and ride calmly to the top. Once there, the dog has to search quickly. A person buried in the snow can suffocate or get dangerously cold very quickly.

Panda runs toward the spot where a person is buried in the snow.

She digs right where the victim's face is.

Most search and rescue dogs need rewards like the chance to play ball or to eat a special treat, but not Newfies. Their reward is finding a person, saving a life. Their joy is obvious as they wag their tails and lick the faces of the people they rescue. No one wants to get lost in the woods or buried in the snow. But if it happens, there is no better way to be rescued than by a big, loving Newfoundland dog.

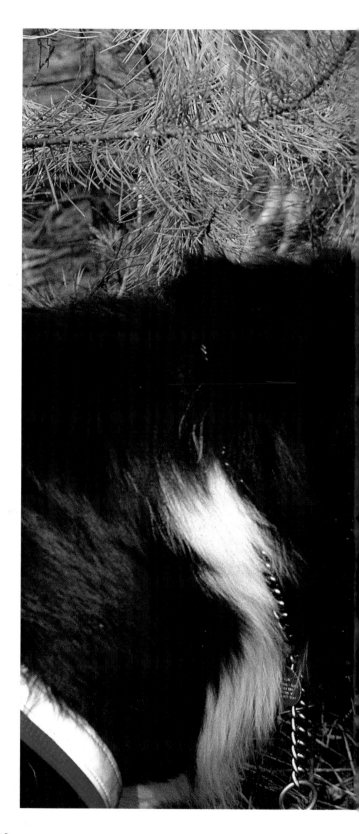

Being "found" by a Newfoundland means getting kissed.